Old PORT GLASGOW
by
Joy Monteith

West Harbour and Fore Street, early 1900s.

© Joy Monteith 2003
First published in the United Kingdom, 2003, by Stenlake Publishing Ltd.
01290 551122
www.stenlake.co.uk

ISBN 9781840332506

Printed by Blissetts, Roslin Road, Acton, W3 8DH

With the exception of those supplied by Inverclyde Libraries and Robert Grieves (see acknowledgements), copies of the pictures featured in this book may be obtained by contacting Kempock Digital Prints, 48 Kempock Street, Gourock, PA19 1ND, 01475 632174, www.kempockdigital.co.uk.

ACKNOWLEDGEMENTS

Thanks are due to many people who helped with information about individual photographs, especially John Sharpe who supplied several of the photographs together with background information. Thanks also to Sandra Macdougall of Inverclyde Libraries and Betty Hendry of the Watt Library for providing assistance with research material, and to Oliver van Helden of Stenlake Publishing for back-up and technical advice.

The publishers would like to thank John Sharpe for his invaluable help in providing additional pictures for this book. Thanks also to John McMorland and Andrew Green, Martin Coyle, Norman Burniston (who gave permission to use the picture on page 11) Robert Grieves (who provided the picture on page 1), Inverclyde Libraries (who provided the pictures on pages 3, 6 (lower), 11, 19, 26 and 29) and the National Library of Scotland Map Library.

FURTHER READING

The publications listed below were used by the author during her research. None of them are available from Stenlake Publishing. Those interested in finding out more are advised to contact their local bookshop or reference library.

Bowie, Janetta, *The Port: Past–Present 1775–1975*
Greenock Telegraph
MacArthur, William, *History of Port Glasgow*
Monteith, Joy & McPherson, Robert, *Port Glasgow and Kilmacolm from Old Photographs*
Port Glasgow Express
Statistical Accounts of the parish of Port Glasgow 1793, 1836, 1962

HMS *Vanguard* was the last and most powerful battleship to be built for the Royal Navy. Ordered in March 1941, she was built at John Browns at Clydebank, and launched by Princess Elizabeth on 30 November 1944. The *Vanguard* represented the pinnacle of battleship design, incorporating amendments which took account of experience gained during World War II, and her armament consisted of eight 15-inch, sixteen 5¼-inch and 71 close range anti-aircraft guns. Her history is unique, however, in that she is the only British battleship never to have fired her guns in anger. Following her entry into service, the *Vanguard* was used to take the royal family on a visit to South Africa in 1947, and in 1949 she joined the Mediterranean Fleet. In 1951 the *Vanguard* became flagship of the Home Fleet. She had a regular complement of 1,600 crew. Latterly, she was placed in the Reserve Fleet until 1960 when the decision was taken for *Vanguard* to be sold; she returned to the Clyde to be scrapped at Faslane between 1960 and 1962. This photograph shows HMS *Vanguard* passing Port Glasgow after being commissioned for trials on 25 April 1946.

INTRODUCTION

Although the history of Port Glasgow goes back no further than the mid-seventeenth century, the story of its growth, development and ability to adapt to change is a remarkable one. It began in 1667 when the magistrates of Glasgow, seeking a deep water port downriver to accommodate increasing trade with the New World, approached Sir Patrick Maxwell of Newark Estate with a request to feu land to provide harbour facilities for the city. At this time the Newark Estate included a small fishing hamlet with a good anchorage and Newark Castle, built between 1450 and 1599. Following negotiations, Sir Patrick leased about thirteen acres of land west of the castle to the City of Glasgow in 1668 at a price of 1,300 merks, or £72 4s 5d, plus an annual feu duty of four merks. As a result 'Newport Glasgow' was constituted a free port and the construction of piers and harbours was started at once.

By 1710 Newport Glasgow was the principal customs house port on the Clyde and the town had extended its original limits so greatly that it had practically absorbed the separate village of Newark. It was 1775, however, before the two villages were officially united as the burgh of Port Glasgow.

By this time Port Glasgow faced major change as the first successful attempts at deepening the Clyde resulted in the gradual shift of trade to Glasgow itself. Whilst Port Glasgow remained the major location for the import of timber, it suffered an inevitable decline as a port. However, the advent of the first shipyard at Newark in 1780 signalled diversification to an activity which would become the principal industry of Port Glasgow for over 200 years.

In due course the entire waterfront from the Greenock boundary on the west to Newark Castle on the east became a continuous line of shipyards, docks and harbours, producing ships which bear honoured names in shipping history. This, together with the associated industries of sailmaking and rope-making, provided employment for thousands of people over the years, and created a massive impact on both the environment and the psyche of Port Glasgow. In addition, rapid industrial growth in the nineteenth century brought attendant problems of difficult housing and social conditions, aggravated by the limited geographical confines of the one square mile of the original town. By the end of the twentieth century all these factors had changed dramatically.

Shipbuilding and its related industries have all but disappeared from Port Glasgow, with the notable exception of the Ferguson Shipyard at Newark where it all began. Changed too are the congested housing conditions within the square mile of the original town, thanks to the remarkable progress achieved in housing provision by the local authority throughout the twentieth century.

The harbours are filled in, and it is easy to speculate that a visitor returning to Port Glasgow today after 50 years or so would find the town unrecognisable. Nonetheless, the landmark of the municipal buildings pinpoints the area of the former harbour, and the grid system of streets still stretches back from the original frontage of Fore Street. Above all, despite the extraordinary changes in the economy and geography of Port Glasgow there remains a strong sense of a closely-knit and generous community united by a unique and distinguished history of growth beside the River Clyde.

Right: The Perch Lighthouse dates from the 1860s when it was constructed to mark a bank of rocks which only became exposed at low tide. It is a cast iron cylindrical structure on a circular stone base, with a triangular-paned lantern with domed top. It also includes iron steps to its doorway. Passing the light is the well-loved paddle steamer, the second *Lord of the Isles*, which entered service in 1891. She was designed and built in Partick, Glasgow for the Glasgow & Inverary Steamboat Company and for many years sailed a daily route from Bridge Wharf to Inverary and back. In 1912 the *Lord of the Isles* was sold to Turbine Steamers Ltd. and placed on a daily cruise round the Isle of Bute to Tighnabruaich. She was withdrawn from service in 1928.

Newark Castle was built by the Maxwell family of Finlaystone over a period of about 150 years. The oldest part of the existing castle was constructed between 1450 and 1477 by Sir John Maxwell, and at this time was known as the 'New Werke of Finlastoun' from which the village of Newark took its name. On at least two occasions – in 1495 and 1497 – King James IV visited Newark from his fortress at Dumbarton. The central portion of the castle was completed about 1597–99 by Sir Patrick Maxwell and above the main entrance is a panel dated 1597 with the monogram PM and the inscription 'The Blissingis of God be Herein'. It was Sir Patrick's son (also Patrick) who feued about thirteen acres of the family's estate to the magistrates of Glasgow in 1668 to provide harbour facilities for the city merchants. This resulted in the formation of 'Newport Glasgow', a free port which was quite separate from the village of Newark until 1775.

Following amalgamation with Port Glasgow in 1775, the area around Newark became a location for shipbuilding. One of the earliest shipbuilders in the area was Thomas McGill who established a yard close to the castle in 1780. By the late nineteenth century Newark Castle had been completely surrounded by shipyards, most famously those of Wm. Hamilton & Co. (before they transferred to the Glen Yard), Ferguson Bros., and Lamont's ship repair works at the Castle Yard. Following the construction of the *Comet* in 1812 at John Wood's yard, local shipbuilding expanded considerably, and by 1910 a contemporary account describes Port Glasgow as having eight large shipbuilding yards along the river front. Four of these yards were on an extensive scale and at Russell's, for example, over 2,000 workers were regularly employed and in one year attained first place in the world for tonnage built. The Ferguson Shipbuilding Yard at Newark Castle is still operating and is the only remaining yard in the Port Glasgow area.

Broadstone House was built between 1869 and 1870 above the cliffs at the easternmost entrance to Port Glasgow. The architect was David Bryce who designed several country baronial mansions throughout Scotland, and Broadstone reputedly included details which were based on Newark Castle. For many years it was the home of John Birkmyre of the Gourock Ropework Company, but from 1929 the building was used for hospital premises when it was bought by the health board from the Birkmyres for £10,000. Broadstone has lain derelict for several years whilst various private housing developments have been mooted, but to date not implemented.

The Moffat or Carnegie Park Orphanage was opened on 19 January 1885. It was funded by a bequest from James Moffat, a local benefactor who had founded the Moffat Library two or three years earlier. James Moffat was a merchant from Greenock who acquired premises in the Port Glasgow Municipal Buildings where he carried out a large trade as a wholesale and retail grocer and wine merchant for 40 years. When he died in 1884 aged 66, he bequeathed his considerable fortune to several charitable institutions in Scotland as well as various local charities. The orphanage could accommodate 30 boys and 30 girls in two separate units and was situated in two acres of ground. The estimated cost at the time for the building and fitting out was £5,000.

For a number of years Carnegie Park Gardens was the only tenemental housing development to the east of Newark Castle on the Glasgow Road. Built before 1913, it was named after James Moffat's Carnegie Estate which he purchased several years before his death with the object of providing a suitable site for his proposed orphanage, plus income from the ground rental of properties on the site to assist with the orphanage's running costs. The properties at Fyfe Park (visible in the distance) were built some time later, probably around the 1920s. The original boundary of the estate was the Carnegie Burn which runs down the east end of Port Glasgow cemetery, roughly along the line of Heggie's Avenue. The cemetery opened in 1859 replacing those at Newark, Blackstone and Port Glasgow churchyard. To the east the housing development at Woodhall Estate was built in 1936 to relieve overcrowding in the town centre.

Newark remained a separate settlement from Port Glasgow until 1775. It was originally established as a fishing village with a few houses for workers on the Newark Estate, and a report of 1655 records 'fore or five houses' together with several crofts. The village developed rapidly in the seventeenth and eighteenth centuries and housing was built all along the frontage of the Bay area. This frontage was quite open to the river, and it has been said that many of the buildings incorporated a pane of glass reputedly to provide light to guide the fishing boats back at night. To the south most of the houses had ample gardens running up to where the railway line was later built. At the end of the nineteenth century, the Medical Officer of Health drew attention to the large number of slum properties in the Bay Street area of the town (above), and suggested that action should be taken under the Housing of the Working Classes Act. Within the area of four and a half acres described as an 'insanitary warren' there were 438 houses with a population of 2,007 persons.

Within the 'insanitary warren' of the Bay area there was a network of closes including Sinclair's Close, Whiteside Close, Guthrie's Close, Salmond Close, Boyd's Close and Well Close. One of the best known was Black Bull Close which was named after the inn which stood on the corner of the lane and Bay Street. Illustrated in these two views, the close had been in existence for over 200 years by the time of the Medical Officer's report, and was part of the original village of Newark. As the town developed the whole area became congested with many 'backland' developments of houses of poor design being built and subdivided during the nineteenth century. Typically the houses had wooden outside stairs and landings and were without water, sanitation and gas. Each landing had a tap which provided the water supply for several houses and homes would be lit by paraffin lamps. On 30 May 1910 a start was made on the demolition of the area around the Black Bull Inn and Close and other properties up to Ropework Lane allowing room for new construction to begin in August.

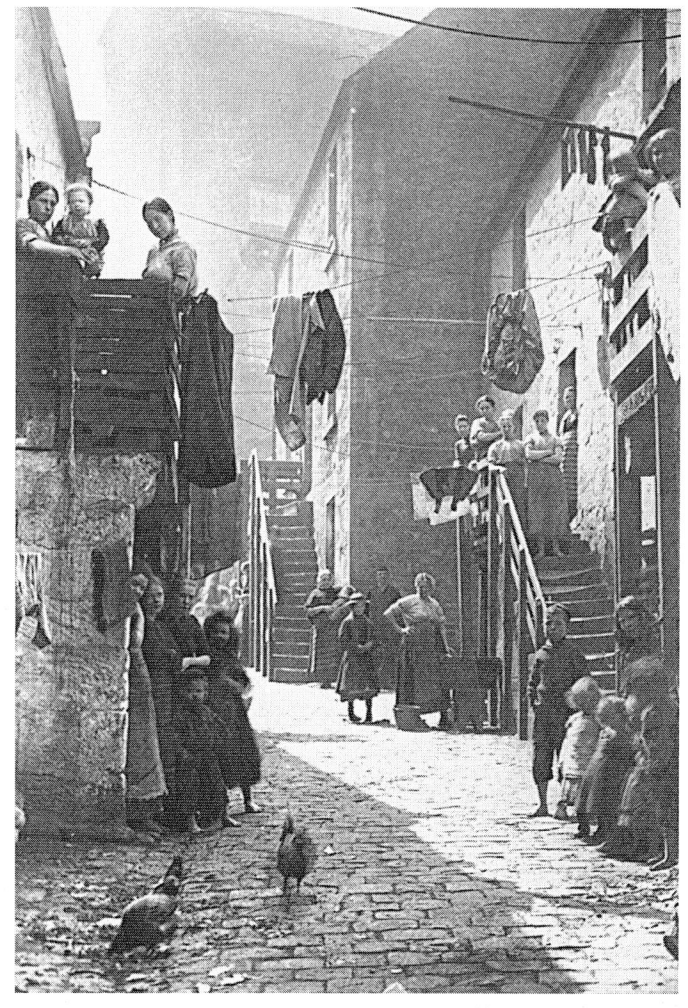

In 1902 W. T. Lithgow made an offer of £10,000 to the town council to help purchase the old buildings in the Bay Street area. Demolition of the entire district began in 1909 and by May 1910 considerable progress had been made, with fourteen substantial red sandstone tenements completed and tenants obtaining possession of their new homes. The entire Bay scheme was completed in 1912 at an estimated cost of £100,000 and consisted of 48 blocks containing 378 houses, 41 shops, two banks and a labour exchange. Prior to these improvements, a notable amenity had already been added to the area by the donation of the Port Glasgow Baths and Washhouses (above, right) in 1894. These were provided through the generosity of shipbuilder Joseph Russell who gave the sum of £5,700 for their construction, and the washhouses in particular were considered a great boon at the time. They closed in 1961 and in 2003 the swimming baths were undergoing a major refurbishment.

Although the Bay area housing scheme which was completed in 1912 constituted a great improvement to the town, the properties were in need of considerable refurbishment by the 1960s. The town council acquired them from the Bay Development Trust with a view to modernising them, but estimates for this work proved too costly and the council eventually decided on redevelopment. This scheme included the construction of Port Glasgow's three fifteen-storey blocks of flats, namely Rowan, Thistle and Heather Courts. Construction began at the end of June 1969, and by February 1970, when this photograph was taken, they were well on the way to completion. The project, which was expected to cost £500,000, comprised 177 houses equally divided between two and three apartments. The ship on the river is the *Baknes* undergoing trials after construction at Scott Lithgow's Cartsburn Yard.

BIRKMYRE ROPE WORK, PORT GLASGOW.

With the development of both shipping and shipbuilding in the area, other support industries such as ropeworks, sailworks, foundries and, later, engineering works were established. The Port Glasgow Rope & Duck Company was set up in 1736 by a group of Glasgow merchants in a mill where the railway station is now situated. In 1797 the company sold their ropeworks and mills to the Gourock Ropework Co., which relocated to Port Glasgow from their premises at Cove Road, Gourock. From then on the business advanced rapidly, especially after 1814 when the Birkmyre family became associated with the firm. The Bay Street mill (above) was originally a sugar refinery, but was rebuilt about 1868 as a massive eight-storey building to produce canvas and sailcloth. Gourock Ropeworks was internationally renowned and manufactured a wide range of goods including sails, cordage, fishing nets, sports nets, tenting and tarpaulin. The company supplied the ropes for the first *Comet* in 1812 and the hawsers for the *Queen Mary* in 1936. The ropeworks finally closed in 1975 and although the main building is still standing the extensive surrounding ropewalks were demolished in 1980.

Before the creation of the roundabout at Blackstone and the realignment of the A8 dual carriageway along the foreshore to the front of Kelburn, all traffic travelling east towards Glasgow as well as to upper Port Glasgow and Kilmacolm had to pass under the railway bridge at the junction of Bay Street and the west end of Robert Street. On the left are buildings belonging to the Gourock Ropeworks complex and on Bay Street a tram is approaching its terminus beside St Mary's Episcopal Church. This church had been gifted in 1854 by Miss Catherine Shaw Stewart who had served with Florence Nightingale in the Crimean War. It was demolished in the 1980s to make way for the new road, and its congregation moved to new premises beside Kilmacolm Road.

This view over the lower part of Clune Brae locates the dominant building of Gourock Ropeworks and the extensive industrial buildings which surrounded it. During the latter part of the nineteenth century many tenements for mill and shipyard workers appeared in the area at Clune Brae, Cairn Terrace, Newark Place and most notably Bouverie Street. The majority of the tenements at Bouverie were built in the 1890s by the Gourock Ropework Co. for their employees. Originally there were 276 houses in the terrace, comprising one or two apartments with outside communal toilets. Many of these houses were damaged in the Blitz of 1941. In 1955 one of the biggest housing improvements ever to be carried out in Scotland up until that time was undertaken at Bouverie when 165 larger, modernised apartments were created from the original number, at an estimated cost of £900 per house.

Described as Clunebraehead, these houses on Clune Brae are situated just before the location of the old toll house at the corner of High Carnegie Road. The properties appear on the 1913 Ordnance Survey map as among some of the very few in the area at that time.

The toll house was situated on Clune Brae approximately where the former Clydeview Roadhouse (now flats) was later built. Tolls were first introduced after the Turnpike Act of 1753 to raise revenue to repair highways, and in 1790–92 a new main road was completed between Port Glasgow and Glasgow. As upper Port Glasgow developed after World War II, the line of Clune Brae and Kilmacolm Road stayed much the same until October 1961 when a major road improvement scheme was proposed for the route to Kilmacolm. The dangerous S-bend was removed and the realignment of the carriageway meant the removal of the toll house plus a manse, two private houses, a doctor's surgery and a cafe at Boglestone where a new roundabout was built. In addition a cul-de-sac was to be formed at the end of the villas on Clune Brae. The scheme was estimated to cost £182,000.

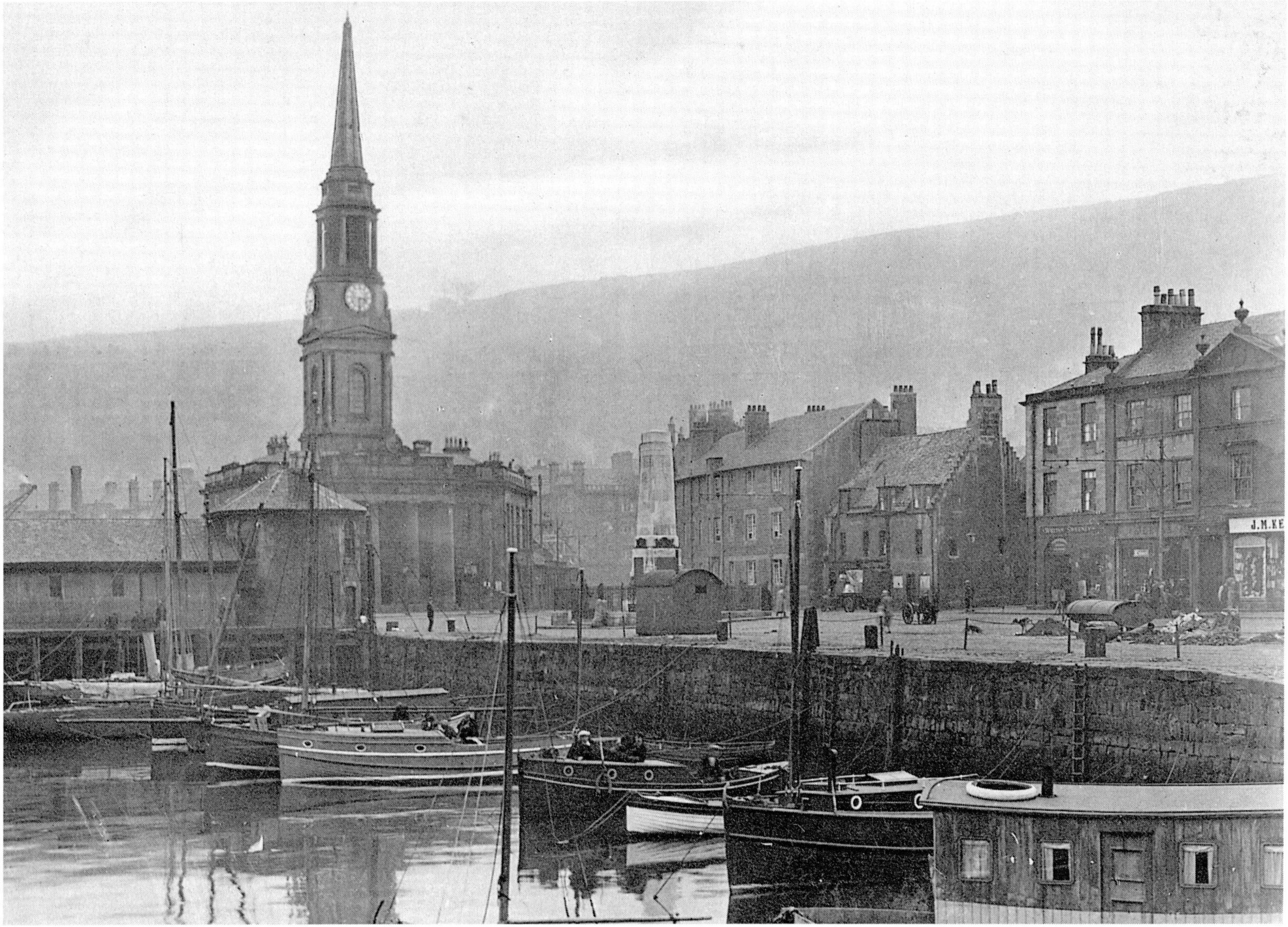
J.M.KE

Opposite: When the thirteen acres of Newark Estate were acquired by the City of Glasgow in 1668 the erection of a pier and docks was set about at once and Newport Glasgow prospered rapidly. There was considerable trade with Virginia, and throughout the eighteenth century trade grew with the West Indies, by which time the prefix 'New' had been dropped from regular usage. At this time the main imports were tobacco, sugar, rum, cotton, mahogany and logwood, together with timber, iron and hemp from the Baltic. Between 86 and 90 ships were entering the harbour from foreign parts every year. Goods were then transported by road from Port Glasgow to the city. At the same time Port Glasgow and Newark were a principal source of vegetables and fruit for Glasgow, with market gardens established on the west side of the town from Balfour Street to Inchgreen, and around Newark Castle and at Carnegie and the foot of Clune Brae.

In the *Statistical Account* of 1836, Port Glasgow's harbour facilities are described as 'two capacious harbours, substantially built, and so completely sheltered from the storm that the vessels moored in them have seldom been found to suffer injury even from the severest weather'. In addition the port was furnished with ample quay and shed rooms and could accommodate vessels of upwards of 600 tons. Throughout the eighteenth century most of the vessels using the port had remained the property of Glasgow merchants, but this changed after 1773 when the successful deepening of the Clyde, allowing vessels to navigate further upriver, resulted in the gradual shift of larger trade to Glasgow itself. Nonetheless, Port Glasgow remained the principal port for the import of timber from North America for which secure and extensive wood-ponds were constructed along the shores. In addition, whilst Port Glasgow's pre-eminence as a port declined at the start of the nineteenth century, its importance as a shipbuilding centre was to develop with the opportunities provided by the Industrial Revolution and the shift from sail to steam.

By the beginning of the twentieth century cargoes had changed and it was becoming less common for timber to be imported at Port Glasgow. For a while iron ore from Europe and pig iron from the North of England were major imports. Gradually however, trade declined, and the west harbour in particular began to silt up. By 1930 Port Glasgow Harbour Trust had accepted an offer of £3,000 from the town council to purchase the harbours as a town improvement. The area covered 99,600 square yards and included a dismantled shipbuilding yard formerly occupied by Lithgow's, and the dry dock, which had been built in 1762 and was the first of its kind in Scotland. The harbour was the berth of the lighthouse and buoy tender the *Torch*, the vessel in this photograph being the one built by Duncan's of Port Glasgow in 1882, and replaced in 1924 by a ship of the same name which was dismantled at Lamont's (Greenock) in 1977.

In 1710 Port Glasgow was constituted the principal custom house port of the Clyde and retained this distinction until 1812 when Greenock and Glasgow were declared independent ports. The first custom house was established in a building in, appropriately, Customhouse Lane. However, with the rapid development of trade, larger premises were required and a new custom house was built on West Quay in 1754. In 1830 for example, the amount of revenue collected at the port was £243,349 3s 1d, although thereafter income declined and in 1895 there were proposals to transfer remaining custom activities to Greenock. The custom house building (second from the right in this picture) remained in use for many years, and was used as premises for the Constitution Club and latterly as a boys' club. Moves to restore the building proved impossible as it had reached such a dilapidated condition, and it was finally demolished in 1965 to accommodate the realignment plans for the A8.

CORONATION PARK, PORT GLASGOW

After the town council bought the harbours, the process of infilling the west section in front of Fore Street continued over a period of several years in the 1930s. When the work was nearing completion in 1935, plans were discussed for using the area as a recreation ground and as a result Coronation Park was formed. It was laid out with swings, a bandstand and several flower beds and was formally opened on 7 August 1937, providing welcome public access to the riverside. Later on, in the 1960s, further sections of the harbour were filled in in preparation for the major scheme of realigning the A8 and the construction of the dual carriageway. As a result Coronation Park was extended further east towards Newark Castle.

Two notable landmarks still visible in Port Glasgow are the war memorial and the municipal buildings. At one time both were right on the waterfront at the harbourside. Port Glasgow was created a burgh in 1775, administered by a council of thirteen (later nine) townspeople to see to the administration of law, revenue and expenditure. The municipal buildings were designed by the prominent Glasgow architect David Hamilton and built in 1815 at a cost of £12,000, replacing old premises in King Street. The building contained the council chambers and town clerk's office plus shops, reading rooms and several offices which were used as counting houses for mercantile businesses. It also contained the courthouse and police station. The former municipal buildings underwent major restoration in 1995 and presently house Port Glasgow Library. The war memorial was officially unveiled on Sunday 23 October 1921, commemorating 319 Port Glasgow men killed in the 1914–18 war. The cost of funding the monument was raised by public appeal. After the Second World War a new screen wall was added behind the memorial, and unveiled on 9 November 1952.

Scarlow Street was originally called Seagate Street, but some time during the nineteenth century the name was changed to Scarlow. One explanation is that 'scar' is the nautical term for a sunken rock and Scarlow Street ran from the lower part of the shore towards the marginally higher ground of Shore Street. Number 28 Scarlow Street was known as Pawn Close and was the office of the Greenock & Port Glasgow Loan Company. At the corner of Scarlow and King Street was the house in which the shipbuilder John Wood was born. John and Charles Wood took over their father's yard in nearby Shore Street on his death in 1811 and proceeded with the contract to build the *Comet* which achieved a place in record books as the first commercially successful steamship in Europe. Wood's yard continued to be renowned for building river steamers and sailing yachts, and also built two ships for Cunard. John Wood retired when he realised that marine engines were becoming too big for wooden frames, not wishing to venture into new designs for iron ships.

In the 50 years between 1841 and 1891, Port Glasgow's population more than doubled from 7,000 to 14,685 people, with many immigrants from Ireland in particular attracted by the prospect of work in the developing industries. By 1931 it had increased again to 21,000. This rapid growth put severe pressure on housing provision, particularly within the limited boundaries of the town. In areas such as Scarlow Street overcrowding and congestion became inevitable, and there were numerous backland developments and subdivisions of properties. It was not uncommon for properties to be numbered by halves, resulting in addresses such as 2½ Scarlow Street. Although the houses were solidly built they were often small, seldom with more than two rooms, and usually without baths or indoor sanitation. After the Second World War surveys revealed that over 1,200 houses in Port Glasgow were classed as overcrowded and drastic action was required. From 1946 onwards the town council undertook bold and major programmes of new housebuilding throughout the town, with the demolition of narrow streets and lanes in the town centre allowing the provision of modern housing, open spaces and improvements to roads. This photograph shows back properties at 13 Scarlow Street.

A horse-drawn tramway service operated by the Greenock & Port Glasgow Tramway Company was first introduced to the town in 1889, allowing transport as far as Ashton in Gourock. Initially the terminus was at Lyon's Lane beside the municipal buildings in Fore Street, but was soon extended to Blackstone Corner at the junction of Bay Street and Robert Street. Electric trams were introduced for public traffic on 3 October 1901 and in 1918 recorded a peak of 16,901,069 passenger journeys. After this, tramway traffic suffered a downturn in business due to the contemporary depression in trade and the effects of local unemployment. These factors, together with the introduction in 1924 of competition from motor buses which had the advantage of greater mobility, resulted in the closure of the tramway system on Monday 15 July 1929. The tram in the photograph is about to turn on to Fore Street at Scarlow Corner, a notoriously windy corner for pedestrians often called Cape Horn.

FUNERAL OF MR. DUNCAN GILLIES.

Duncan Gillies was a veteran of the Crimean War and the Indian Mutiny who lived for 35 years in Port Glasgow. A native of Glendaruel, he enlisted in the Cameron Highlanders where he served for 21 years before leaving with the highest commendation. On retirement from the army, he and his wife settled at 3 Belhaven Street in Port Glasgow, and he was employed as the gateman at Murdoch & Murray's shipyard for many years. When he died aged 84 on 16 May 1913 arrangements were made for Mr Gillies to be buried with full military honours. His coffin was conveyed on a gun carriage provided by the 3rd Highland (Howitzer) Brigade, accompanied by a firing party and band from the 5th Argyll and Sutherland Highlanders and a representative from Mr Gillies's old regiment. This photograph, looking from the roof of the municipal buildings along Fore Street, was taken on the day of the funeral, Tuesday 20 May 1913.

The shop in this photograph was situated on the south side of the municipal buildings in Fore Street where the public library now stands, and originally belonged to James Moffat, the benefactor of the Moffat Orphanage (see page 6) and other charitable bequests. He also owned a sailing ship called the *Bruce* which brought wines and spirits from Portugal and France – a risky business in the days of sail, and he would often pace the front steps of the buildings waiting for his cargo to arrive. James Addison worked for Mr Moffat as a shop assistant, and took over the business from him when he retired. In due course James Addison moved to new premises which he built across the street in Balmoral Buildings at 11 & 13 Fore Street. He built several other properties in the town, all named after royal palaces or castles, e.g. Buckingham Terrace and Osborne (the family home) at Alderwood Road, and Sandringham Terrace at the Glen. Prior to the move to Osborne the family lived in Lyon's Lane, close to the shop premises.

In September 1676 a contract was given to John Clark, mason, of Glasgow, to build a bulwark at Newport Glasgow along the front of what became known as Fore Street. At this time the area was a sandy bay, and the ground on which the war memorial and the municipal buildings now stand was the beach. As the harbours and quays became established, Fore Street became the main commercial street of the town on the harbour front, with shops, businesses and hotels. Two stagecoaches a day travelling between Greenock and Glasgow stopped for passengers at the King's Arms Hotel in Fore Street. The section of the street shown in this photograph was also known as Dockhead Street, after Port Glasgow's graving dock, the first to be built in Scotland in 1762. Situated behind the municipal buildings, it was lengthened in 1834 and remained in active use up until 1966 when it was operated by James Lamont & Co. However, all traces of the dock have vanished, and the area is now covered by the car park at the health centre.

John Wood Street was typical of the extensive development which comprised the Bay area scheme completed in 1912, and included houses, shops, pubs, banks and the new Star Hotel. Dwelling house accommodation consisted of 35 single apartments, 329 two-apartment houses, six three-apartment dwellings with bathroom and eight four-apartment houses and bathrooms. Whilst John Wood Street has survived, having been refurbished in 1972, much of the area including Bay Street, George Street, Victoria Street and Station Road was cleared again in the 1960s and the housing partly replaced by the high flats. An early flier for the new Star Hotel advertises table d'hôte luncheons at one shilling and sixpence, breakfasts from one shilling upwards and teas from sixpence upwards, with special terms for dining by the week or longer. This building replaced the original Star Hotel which had opened on the same site in 1870 with a dinner for the provost and magistrates provided by the owner Mr Shaw. The old building contained three parlours, a smoking room and eight bedrooms all furnished in 'first-class style'.

The launch of the *Comet* in July 1812 at Charles and John Wood's yard was of major importance in the establishment of Port Glasgow as a renowned location for shipbuilding. Financed by Henry Bell to encourage passenger trips between Glasgow, Port Glasgow and Greenock to his hotel in Helensburgh, the *Comet* was the first commercial steamship to ply in open waters, and her economy and popularity encouraged the rapid development of steam-powered ships. The original vessel was wrecked off Oban in 1820. To mark the significance of the *Comet* to the town, extensive celebrations were held on the centenary of the launch in 1912, including a large procession which was watched by tens of thousands of spectators. An account of the time remarks that 'it was something to be remembered to see the procession enter the new John Wood Street from Princes Street'. A 150th anniversary commemoration was also held in 1962 when a replica of the *Comet* was launched at Lithgow's and sailed with a complement of passengers in nineteenth century dress on her original route to Helensburgh. This replica is now situated in the car park at Shore Street close to where Wood's shipyard was located.

A railway service first arrived in Port Glasgow in March 1841 with the opening of the Caledonian Railway Company's Glasgow, Paisley & Greenock Railway, built at a cost of £814,000. Fares between Port Glasgow and Glasgow were 2s 3d first class, 1s 4d third class with seats, and 1s third class without seats, but the carriages were fitted with a strong bar to prevent passengers falling when the train gave a jolt. The original station was fairly basic, and in 1858 various improvements were introduced and a wooden bridge built across the line to increase the comfort and safety of passengers, who prior to this had often to cross the rails in perilous conditions.

Extensive alterations were carried out to the original station building during 1913/14, sweeping away the small, dark booking office, the ancient waiting rooms and the bookstall under the bridge. The up platform was extended, new offices were installed on the down platform, and more modern waiting rooms were built, plus an island platform for local trains on the left of the down line. In addition, an extended covered entrance was made from Princes Street. The improvements cost £20,000 and the spacious new structure was considered to be one of the finest stations on the 'True Line', namely the Caledonian Railway system.

When Jean Street School (pages 40 and 41) became too small for the expanding needs in secondary education, this new higher grade school was built at Highholm. Opened in November 1909, a special feature of the school was its higher grade department which was equipped with the most modern facilities, including laboratory, art room, cookery room, workshop and drill hall. Pupils from all schools under the local school board who passed the qualifying examination at the age of twelve could transfer to Highholm School where two main courses were open to them – a 'supplementary course' for those whose school life closed at fourteen, and a 'higher grade course' for those who intended to continue at school for about a year longer. The goal of the higher grade course was the Intermediate Certificate which was designed for children who intended to enter the teaching profession or the civil service, or who hoped to embark on a skilled trade or commercial career.

Princes Street from Station, Port Glasgow

From its early days, Port Glasgow was laid out on a grid system with straight streets crossing each other at right angles. By 1832 when the town became a parliamentary burgh, the main streets were already Fore Street, with Church Street leading up to King Street and Princes Street (above). Princes Street contained many shops and businesses including several grocers and spirit dealers, a restaurant, a milliners, and a china shop. Number 63 was the residence of Captain William Hamilton, a retired ship-owner who left his house to be used as a manse, plus money to assist in the building of a church which was named after him and opened in 1848 beside the site later used for the town hall. Further up the street, nearer the station, Princes Street Church was opened in March 1866, having been built at a cost of £2,927. The church closed in 1972 and the building has since been demolished.

TOWN HALL AND PRINCES STREET, PORT GLASGOW

The town council first discussed proposals for a town hall in 1865 but it was another three years before the idea was taken up as a project by the provost of the time, Alexander Lang. As a result the foundation stone for the hall at the foot of Princes Street was laid in 1869 attended by great public celebrations, including a procession of local trades and a public dinner. The town hall opened in 1873 and was used regularly for civic functions as well as productions by visiting drama companies and variety concerts – for example, Harry Lauder visited frequently before he became famous. An organ was donated to the hall by Andrew Carnegie in 1900. By the 1950s the original town hall was becoming unattractive and uncomfortable, and the decision was taken to demolish the old building and replace it with a modern structure on the same site. The new town hall, offering well-appointed and spacious accommodation, was opened in February 1964.

Church Street was named after the parish church first erected on this site in 1717, and in a survey of 1729 was listed as Kirk Street. Port Glasgow first had a minister in 1696 who held services in a sail loft on ground beside the harbour until the new premises seating 800 persons were built in 1717. In 1719 the magistrates of Glasgow paid the costs of seating the loft in the aisle facing the pulpit 'for the magistrates and inhabitants of Glasgow'. By 1767 the parish church had become inadequate for the population and a chapel of ease, later known as Newark Parish Church, was erected in the suburbs in 1774. The church in this photograph was built in 1823 with accommodation for 1,260 people including 50 free sittings for the poor. The stipend of the minister was fixed at £250 with £27 yearly for a house and £3 for a garden.

36

Opposite: This view of Church Street looks in the opposite direction to the previous one, towards the war memorial. Church Street was one of the other main shopping streets of Port Glasgow, and in the early part of the twentieth century shops would be open until 10.00 p.m. The range of shops included grocers, shoemakers, drapers, tobacconists, spirit dealers, fleshers, a printer and a watchmaker. On the left in this photograph is Johnstone's pawn shop while further down the street on the right was Dickson's outfitters who could supply a range of goods including tile hats. They also had a shop in the Bay area. It has been suggested that the horse and carriage in the photograph was operated by the Little Sisters of the Poor who worked regularly in the area providing assistance to poor families. With the exception of the church after which the street was named, all properties in the street have been replaced by developments of the 1930s and 1950s.

As a result of the nature of Port Glasgow's rapid development behind the harbours, housing was always a major problem. The natural features of the land limited the old town to approximately one square mile, resulting in narrow, congested streets, and numerous backland developments with a lack of natural ventilation and sunlight, poor water supply and inadequate sanitary conditions. The back court at 24 Church Street was typical of these poor housing conditions. When twentieth century surveys recommended population densities of 90 people to the acre, Port Glasgow was discovered to have 500 persons. The town council became very active in addressing the problem and new housing estates were built at Chapelton and Woodhall in the 1920s and 30s to relieve congestion. However, it was not until after 1946, when areas such as Devol, Bardrainney, Broadfield and Park Farm were included within the town's new boundaries, that the most remarkable progress was made in provision of housing. This activity coincided with the establishment in 1947 of the industrial estate in the upper part of the town, and by 1953 1,000 new houses had been completed. Between then and 1975 a further 3,300 houses were built; throughout the same period the council undertook major improvements and upgrading of properties in the old town centre.

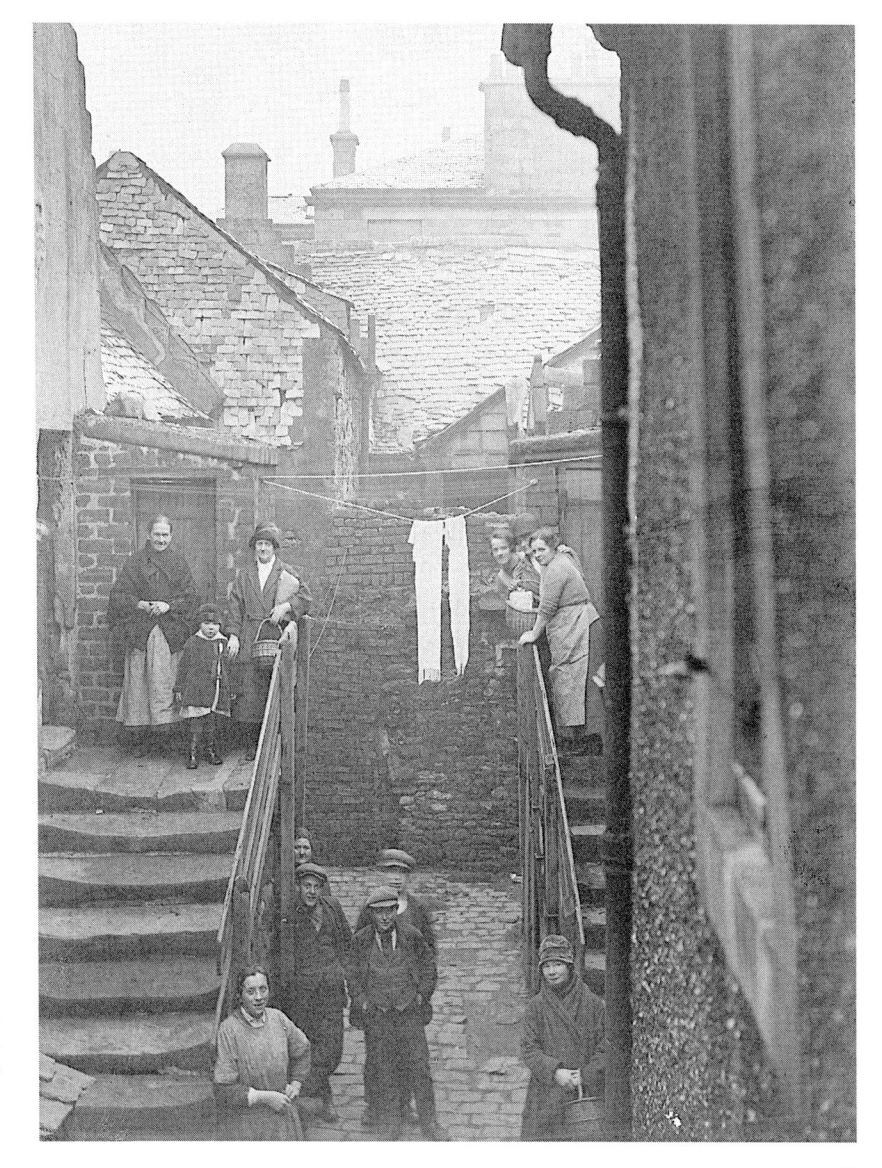

This view of Chapel Lane looks east towards Princes Street and shows the wall at the rear of St John's Church with a lion sculpture on top. The area is now occupied by Huntly Terrace and Place. In a survey of 1836 it was recorded that 332 Roman Catholics lived in the community, served by a priest from Greenock. However, in 1846 Father John Carolan was appointed to Port Glasgow, and by 1854 St John's Church on Shore Street had been built to serve the increasing congregation. In September 1891 a hall in Chapel Lane was opened by His Grace the Archbishop of Glasgow as premises for the League of the Cross. This local branch had over 1,000 members who professed total abstinence from alcoholic drinks, and also promoted thrift and charity amongst the community.

Back Row Lane (right) ran down from Chapel Lane towards the main road at Shore Street, between Princes Street and St John's Church. St John's School was built in association with the Roman Catholic Church in 1883 a short distance west of the lane at the corner of Balfour Street. A commemorative stone was laid by Archbishop Eyre in March 1883 when the building was almost half complete, and the school opened later with accommodation for 800 children. The school building was demolished almost 100 years later in January 1983, with pupils transferring to the new St John's School in Mary Street.

Chapel Lane (left) was named after a chapel of ease accommodating 1,800 people which was built in 1774 in what were then the suburbs; it later became known as Newark Parish Church. In 1836 the minister of this chapel had a stipend of £100 per annum. During the nineteenth century there was a tan works in the lane situated just behind St John's Church, and it was also the location for the stables of the Clyde Iron Company. The advertisement for electric light confirms that after considerable opposition by some residents, electricity supply was introduced to Port Glasgow from Dellingburn in Greenock in 1914 via a sub-station at Boundary Street. At the switching on ceremony on 4 November it was declared that the utility would benefit not just domestic users, but also shipbuilding and other industries, which would have a constant, reliable source of energy from electricity. Gaslight had been introduced in 1829 but initially was only supplied during the hours of darkness. The cost of one gas light used until 11.00 p.m. was 22 shillings per annum.

Port Glasgow School Board had acquired ground in Jean Street as early as 1875 to provide new school accommodation in the area. However there was considerable opposition to the proposal from First Ward residents who considered that their rates were already too high. Nonetheless the project finally went ahead and Jean Street School was officially opened on Saturday 8 November 1884. The architects were W. & D. Barclay and the building was modelled on a recent school in Pollokshields designed by the same firm. On its completion at a cost of £7,000, Jean Street School was considered to be the finest school in the West of Scotland with extensive playgrounds on an admirable site. The original building accommodated 716 pupils on two storeys, and replaced schools at Princes Street and Bouverie Terrace.

At the opening of Jean Street School, the chairman of the school board hoped 'that the comfort and cheerfulness of the school, and the order and cleanliness which would be the rule would be reflected on scholars and their homes, and make real social progress in the community'. By 1898 a third storey had been added to the building to provide accommodation for secondary pupils. Eventually, Jean Street School became too small for the expanding needs of secondary education and a Higher Grade School was built at Highholm in 1908/09 (see page 32). Jean Street finally closed in 1978, when pupils were transferred to Highholm Primary School. The building lay empty for many years until it was refurbished in the 1990s as a number of residential flats called School Court.

As Port Glasgow expanded throughout the eighteenth and nineteenth centuries, the majority of housing was concentrated around the immediate harbour area in narrow and congested conditions. However, many of the ship-owners, industrialists and shipbuilders moved to the rural suburbs and built house such as Rossbank, Glenpark and Marchmont on the western side of the town. For example, Anderson Rodger, shipbuilder, rebuilt Glenpark and lived there from 1882 to 1912; Westvale was the home of James Moffat, merchant and ship-owner; while Marchmont was owned by Joseph Russell of Russell & Co. shipbuilders. The railway line in the photograph was the upper or 'high' line of the Glasgow & South Western Railway, extended from Bridge of Weir to Kilmacolm and down to Greenock at Princes Pier. The line opened to passenger traffic in December 1869. At one time there was a proposal for a station to be opened in upper Port Glasgow near Boglestone, but this was never developed as access was considered too inconvenient for the general community. Passenger services were withdrawn from this line in January 1959.

The Nine Arches was a spectacular sandstone viaduct built in the late 1860s to carry the Glasgow & South Western Railway's Kilmacolm to Princes Pier line across Devol Glen. The name Devol was originally spelt Davol which was thought to be akin to the Gaelic *diabhoul*, meaning 'the evil one'. Nonetheless in a newspaper article of 1920 Devol Glen was described as a local beauty spot to rival many tourist attractions, and was certainly popular for summer walks. Following the closure of the railway line, the viaduct was blown up by the army on 31 October 1970. For about two months beforehand over 70 men worked at weekends erecting scaffolding, and drilling over 200 holes in the piers of the bridge in preparation for the demolition of the 10,000-ton structure. The explosion at 3.00 p.m. caused one broken window in a house nearby.

Lilybank was not laid out until the very end of the nineteenth century when housing in the rural suburbs was built for families of local businessmen and professional people such as solicitors, bankers, merchants and managers in the shipyards and associated industries. In 1897 there were about a dozen houses in the street, situated next to the Gothic-style building of Chapelton School. This was the first school to be built by the school board following the Education Act of 1872. Considered by some residents to be too far from the centre of the town, the school opened in July 1877 at a cost of £4,000 with accommodation for 50 pupils. By 1909 the school roll was 500.

It is possible that Farquhar Road was named after Robert Farquhar, a London banker who bought the Newark Estate from Lord Belhaven in 1820, and whose daughter Eliza Mary married Sir Michael Shaw Stewart of Ardgowan Estate. The Shaw Stewarts in turn became the owners of Newark Castle until it was handed over to the Crown in 1909. Farquhar Road first appears on local maps of the early part of the twentieth century when there were still only a few houses at the western boundary of the town.

Broadstone Hospital, Port Glasgow.

To commemorate their golden wedding anniversary in 1905, Mr and Mrs John Birkmyre of Broadstone House and the Gourock Ropeworks offered to provide a cottage hospital for the town. As a result Broadstone Jubilee Hospital opened in 1907 at a cost of about £35,000, equipped with 25 beds for the treatment of accidents and emergencies. An endowment fund was also set up to assist with the running costs in the era before the introduction of the National Health Service. Broadstone Hospital continued in use until 1979 when hospital services were transferred to Inverclyde Royal Hospital in Greenock. The site is now occupied by Broadstone Gardens sheltered housing complex.

The original western boundary of Port Glasgow was Devol Burn. As the population grew an extension of the burgh was agreed in 1865, allowing Port Glasgow to spread westwards to the point later known as Boundary Street. At the same time the eastern boundary was extended to Heggie's Avenue. In 1927 Greenock applied to Parliament for powers to extend its boundaries to include both Gourock and Port Glasgow. Port Glasgow Council fought vigorously against the proposal and the attempt was defeated. This photograph was taken at the time to show the boundary between Greenock and Port Glasgow. It also shows several streets which have disappeared including Argyle, Octavia and Houston Streets. The housing development at Chapelton (foreground) was the first to be built under the 1919 and 1924 (Assisted) Housing Schemes. On the river frontage is the expanse of the Kingston shipbuilding yard, purchased in 1882 by Joseph Russell, Anderson Rodger and William Todd Lithgow. It was to become the largest yard on the Clyde, and in 1891 Lithgow became the sole owner.

Ardgowan Street, Port Glasgow.

Ardgowan Street was named after the Shaw Stewarts' Ardgowan Estate and was the first part of the main thoroughfare into Port Glasgow running from the Greenock boundary to the Glen Bridge. By the early part of the twentieth century it was a busy location with a considerable number of tenement properties and a variety of shops and businesses, including Morrison's Wine Vaults and the West End Bar. Beside these two premises were the offices of the Port Glasgow & Newark Sailcloth Company, founded in 1843, and further west were the offices of the Kingston Yard. In 1974 the majority of tenements in the area were demolished to accommodate proposals to extend the shipyards, allowing bigger vessels to be built. However, these developments did not take place and in the subsequent realignment of the A8 the remaining stretch of Ardgowan Street was by-passed.

At 14 Ardgowan Street Bailie Robert Rodger carried out a baker's and grocer's business in the shops on either side of the entrance to the close known as Rodger's Close. The small houses behind the close (illustrated here), which stretched down towards the river, were known as Rodger's Court and backed on to the Port Glasgow & Newark Sailcloth Company's ropework buildings. This was a smaller company independent of the Gourock Ropeworks, but which manufactured a similar range of products from yacht sails to mailbags, groundsheets and tarpaulins. In the 1950s the two ropeworks employed ve percent of the working population of Port Glasgow between them, with women outnumbering men by five to two.